Presented to

Carly Adamson
For Attending
Rossland Playgroup
1991 - 1992 Session

HIGHWAY PUBLISHING, EXETER. 0392 77277. PRINTED IN GREAT BRITAIN

D1187759

This well-known fairytale is delightfully illustrated
and simply retold to entertain all young listeners.

Titles in Series S852
Cinderella
Three Little Pigs
Goldilocks and the Three Bears
Jack and the beanstalk
Snow White and the Seven Dwarfs
These titles are also available as a Gift Box set

British Library Cataloguing in Publication Data
Murdock, Hy
    Goldilocks and the three bears. — (Fairy tales. Series 852; 3)
    I. Title   II. Grundy, Lynn N.   III. Series
    823'.914[J]   PZ8
    ISBN 0-7214-9528-1

First Edition

© LADYBIRD BOOKS LTD MCMLXXXV
© Illustrations LYNN N GRUNDY MCMLXXXV
All rights reserved. No part of this publication may be reproduced, stored in a retrieval
system, or transmitted in any form or by any means, electronic, mechanical, photo-copying,
recording or otherwise, without the prior consent of the copyright owners.

Goldilocks and the Three Bears

written by HY MURDOCK
illustrated by LYNN N GRUNDY

Ladybird Books Loughborough

Once upon a time there were Three
Bears who lived in a house in the
woods. There was Father Bear
who was huge and Mother Bear who
was middle-sized and Baby Bear
who was tiny. They all had their own
bowls for their porridge, their own
chairs to sit on and their own
beds to sleep in.

One day, after Mother Bear had made the porridge, they went for a walk while the porridge was cooling.

While the Bears were away, a little girl called Goldilocks came by and looked through the window into their house.

Goldilocks was a naughty little girl
and the next thing she did was to
open the door and go into the house.

There on the table were three bowls of porridge. Goldilocks tasted the porridge in the big bowl but that was too hot. Next she tasted the porridge in the middle-sized bowl and that was too cold. But when she tasted the porridge in the little bowl, it was just right and Goldilocks ate it all up.

Then Goldilocks looked around the room
She saw the three chairs. When she sat
in the biggest chair she found it was too
hard for her.

Next she sat in the middle-sized chair and that was much too soft. Then she sat in the smallest chair and she found that it felt just right. But this little chair wasn't strong enough to hold Goldilocks. It broke!... And Goldilocks landed with a bump on the floor.

Next this naughty little girl wondered what else she could find and she decided to go upstairs. There she saw the three beds and, because by now

she was beginning to feel tired, she lay down on the very big bed. This bed was much too hard so she tried the middle-sized bed. That was much too soft and so she went and lay on the smallest bed. That was just right. Goldilocks curled up and soon she was fast asleep.

By now the Bears were hungry for their porridge and they went home. But when they went inside their house they knew someone had been there.

"Who's been eating my porridge?" said Father Bear, in his huge, gruff voice.

"Who's been eating my porridge?" said Mother Bear, in her middle-sized voice.

"Someone's been eating my porridge and they've eaten it all up!" cried Baby Bear in his tiny, squeaky voice.

Then they looked around the room.
"Someone's been sitting in my chair," said Father Bear.

"Someone's been sitting in my chair," said Mother Bear.

"Someone's been sitting in my chair... and they've broken it!" shouted Baby Bear.

The Bears thought they had better
search the rest of the house and so they
went upstairs.
The Three Bears looked around.

"Who's been lying in my bed?"
roared Father Bear, in his huge, gruff voice.

"Who's been lying in my bed?" asked Mother Bear, in her middle-sized voice.

But when Baby Bear looked at his bed, he cried out in his tiny, squeaky voice, **"Someone's been lying in my bed... and she's still there!"**

The sound of voices woke Goldilocks.
She sat up in bed and saw the Three
Bears looking at her. She was so
surprised that she jumped out of bed,
ran down the stairs and out of the
door, as fast as she could, and away
into the woods.

The Three Bears started to chase after her but the naughty Goldilocks had gone. They never saw her again and the Three Bears lived happily ever after.